United States Presidents

Andrew Johnson

Anne Welsbacher
ABDO Publishing Company

visit us at
www.abdopub.com

Published by ABDO Publishing Company, 4940 Viking Drive, Edina, Minnesota 55435.
Copyright © 2000 by Abdo Consulting Group, Inc. International copyrights reserved in all countries. No part of this book may be reproduced in any form without written permission from the publisher.

Printed in the United States.

Cover and Interior Photo credits: Archive Photos, UPI/Corbis-Bettmann

Contributing editors: Robert Italia, Tamara L. Britton, K. M. Brielmaier, Kate A. Furlong
Book design/maps: Patrick Laurel

Library of Congress Cataloging-in-Publication Data

Welsbacher, Anne, 1955-
     Andrew Johnson / Anne Welsbacher.
         p. cm. -- (United States presidents)
      Includes index.
     Summary: Follows the life and career of the statesman who became the seventeenth president of the United States after the assassination of Abraham Lincoln.
      ISBN 1-57765-240-1
      1. Johnson, Andrew, 1808-1875--Juvenile literature.
     2. Presidents--United States--Biography--Juvenile literature.
     [1. Johnson, Andrew, 1808-1875. 2. Presidents.] I. Title.
     II. Series: United States presidents (Edina, Minn.)
     E667.W45   1999
     973.8'1'092--dc21
      [B]   98-21104
                                                                CIP
                                                                 AC

Contents

Andrew Johnson

*A*ndrew Johnson was the seventeenth president of the United States. He was vice president under President Abraham Lincoln. He became president in 1865 after the **Civil War** ended, when Lincoln was shot and killed.

As president, Andrew Johnson tried to follow the rules of the Constitution. He favored states' rights. But the U.S. **Congress** did not always agree with his decisions. Congress felt that Johnson misused his power.

Andrew Johnson was the first president to be **impeached**. A trial was held in Congress to decide if he had broken the law. Then Congress voted to decide if he should be removed from office. Johnson stayed in office by only one vote.

Andrew Johnson was president for four years. Later, he became the only former president elected to the U.S. Senate. Johnson died in 1875.

President Andrew Johnson

Andrew Johnson (1808-1875)
Seventeenth President

BORN:	December 29, 1808
PLACE OF BIRTH:	Raleigh, North Carolina
ANCESTRY:	Scots-Irish, English
FATHER:	Jacob Johnson (1778-1812)
MOTHER:	Mary "Polly" McDonough Johnson (1783-1856)
WIFE:	Eliza McCardle (1810-1876)
CHILDREN:	Five: 3 boys, 2 girls
EDUCATION:	Self-taught
RELIGION:	No formal affiliation
OCCUPATION:	Tailor
MILITARY SERVICE:	Brigadier general
POLITICAL PARTY:	Democratic; elected vice president on National Union ticket

OFFICES HELD:	Councilman; mayor of Greeneville, Tennessee; member of Tennessee legislature, member of U.S. House of Representatives, governor of Tennessee, U.S. senator, vice president
AGE AT INAUGURATION:	56
YEARS SERVED:	1865-1869
VICE PRESIDENT:	None
DIED:	July 31, 1875, Carter Station, Tennessee, age 66
CAUSE OF DEATH:	Stroke

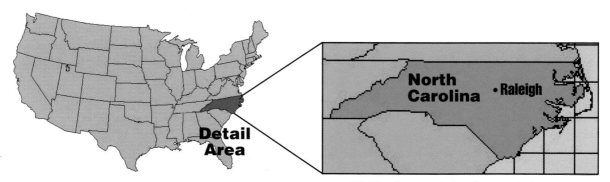

Birthplace of Andrew Johnson

Early Life

*A*ndrew Johnson was born on December 29, 1808, in Raleigh, North Carolina. The Johnson family was very poor. His father, Jacob, worked at an inn. His mother, Polly, was a spinner and weaver. Andy had one brother.

In 1811, Andy's father jumped into a cold lake to save a drowning man. Jacob became sick and died. Later, Andy's mother married again. But the family still had little money. They could not afford to send Andy to school.

Andy enjoyed playing, swimming, and hunting. Many times he was the leader in his group of friends. He was cheerful, and he helped his mother chop wood and do other chores.

Andrew Johnson's birthplace in Raleigh, North Carolina

Tailor's Apprentice

Andrew Johnson became an **apprentice** to a **tailor** when he was 14. He agreed to work for James Selby until he was 21.

While Johnson sewed, another worker read aloud to him. Johnson listened to stories, books about history, and even the Constitution. In this way, he became better educated.

When Johnson was 16, he and some other boys ran away. It was illegal for an apprentice to leave his job, so James Selby offered a reward for Johnson's return.

Johnson traveled from town to town in North Carolina. But no one would hire an escaped apprentice. And he was always in danger of being caught.

For a while, Johnson ran his own tailor shop. Then he returned home to buy his freedom from James Selby. But Selby refused to release Johnson from his contract.

To avoid arrest, Johnson decided to leave North Carolina. In 1826, Johnson and his family moved to Greeneville, Tennessee. Soon, he met Eliza McCardle.

Andrew Johnson's tailor shop in Greeneville, Tennessee

Johnson's Family

*I*n March 1827, Johnson opened a **tailor** shop. On May 17, 1827, he married Eliza. They had five children: Martha, Charles, Mary, Robert, and Andrew.

Johnson was a good tailor. Many people came to his shop. They sat and discussed politics and slavery while he worked. Tennessee was a slave state. Many rich farmers owned slaves.

Johnson became a good speaker and **debater**. He decided to become involved in politics.

Opposite page:
Eliza Johnson

The Making of the Seventeenth United States President

1808 → Born December 29 in Raleigh, North Carolina

1811 → Father dies

1822 → Becomes tailor's apprentice

1826 → Family moves to Greeneville, Tennessee

1835 → Elected to Tennessee House of Representatives

1841 → Elected to Tennessee Senate

1843 → Elected to U.S. House of Representatives

1853 → Elected governor of Tennessee

1864 → Named vice president by Lincoln

1865 Civil War ends; Lincoln assassinated; Johnson becomes president

1866 Freedmen's Bureau Act, Civil Rights Bill passed by Congress

1867 Congress passes Reconstruction Acts and Tenure of Office Bill

PRESIDENTIAL

Andrew Johnson

"It is our sacred duty to transmit unimpaired to our posterity the blessings of liberty which were bequeathed to us by the founders of the Republic..."

1827
Marries Eliza McCardle

1829
Elected Greeneville councilman

1831
Elected mayor of Greeneville

Historic Events
during Johnson's Presidency

Nebraska admitted to the Union

Commercial typewriter invented by Christopher L. Sholes

Alice's Adventures in Wonderland by Lewis Carroll is published

1857
Elected to U.S. Senate

1861
Civil War begins; Tennessee secedes from the Union

1862
Appointed military governor of Tennessee

1868
Impeached by Congress; acquitted by one vote

1869
Presidential term ends; returns to Tennessee

1872
Runs for Tennessee Senate but loses

1875
Elected to U.S. Senate; dies July 31

YEARS

Johnson in Politics

*I*n 1829, Johnson was elected to the town council of Greeneville. On the council, Johnson spoke about rights for poor and working-class people.

In 1831, Johnson was elected the mayor of Greeneville. He served three terms. He was elected to the Tennessee **House of Representatives** in 1835.

Johnson became known for his energetic speeches. He kept working for the rights of laborers. And he fought wasteful government spending.

Johnson was elected to the Tennessee state senate in 1841. Two years later, Johnson became a member of the U.S. House of Representatives. He served in the House for ten years.

During that time, Johnson tried to pass a homestead bill. The bill would give land in the West to settlers and farmers. Southern politicians defeated the bill. Many were wealthy landowners. They did not want the country giving land away.

Johnson defended the rights of workers and the poor. He also argued for the constitutional rights of states to govern themselves. And he proposed many laws that limited the **federal** government's power over the states.

In 1853, Johnson became governor of Tennessee. He helped start a public school system and public library for the state. He was re-elected in 1855.

Andrew Johnson was a mayor, senator, and governor.

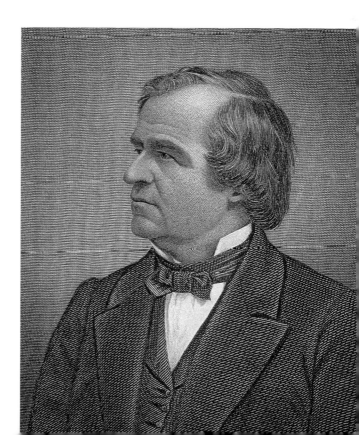

The Loyal Senator

*I*n 1857, Johnson was elected to the U.S. Senate. By now, slavery had become a big problem. Northerners wanted to end it. But Southerners wanted to keep it. Johnson continued to support states' rights to allow slavery. And he kept fighting for his homestead bill. It became law in 1862.

In November 1860, Abraham Lincoln was elected president. A few weeks later, many Southern states **seceded** from the **Union**. They feared President Lincoln would end slavery. They called their new country the **Confederate** States of America.

Johnson was a Southerner and a slave owner. But he also felt secession was unconstitutional. He told the Senate he was a "Union man." He was the only Southern senator to remain in the U.S. **Congress**.

The **Civil War** began on April 12, 1861. A few days later, Tennessee joined the Confederacy. But Union forces slowly gained control of the state.

In March 1862, President Lincoln made Johnson the military governor of Tennessee. Johnson moved to Nashville to set up a state government. His family stayed behind.

Johnson's family became trapped by **Confederate** soldiers. For almost a year, Johnson did not know if they were alive. But in 1863, his family made it to Nashville.

In 1864, Lincoln chose Andrew Johnson to be his vice president. Lincoln wanted a Southern vice president to show the country that the **federal** government represented everyone.

Before the **Civil War** ended, **Congress** formed the **Freedmen's** Bureau. It gave food, medicine, and an education to African Americans in the South.

The well-supplied North won the Civil War's final battles. On April 9, 1865, the South surrendered.

THE UNION

THE CONFEDERACY

President Johnson

*O*n April 14, 1865, actor John Wilkes Booth shot President Lincoln to **avenge** the South. Lincoln died the next day. By law, Vice President Johnson was now president.

It was Johnson's task to bring the Southern states back into the **Union**. This is called **Reconstruction**.

President Johnson favored an easy and smooth reunion. In May 1865, he announced his Reconstruction plan.

Each Southern state could return if it wrote a new state constitution. Each state also had to elect a new governor and **repeal** its act of **secession**. And each state had to approve the Thirteenth **Amendment**, which outlawed slavery. Johnson also pardoned all Southerners except some military and government leaders.

By the fall of 1865, every Southern state had re-entered the Union. Many of the "new" Southern state leaders had held

The United States during Johnson's presidency

power in the South before the **Civil War**. They passed laws
called black codes.

Black codes limited the rights of the **freedmen**. They could
only be laborers or farm workers. They could not own
weapons. And they could not vote.

Many Northern congressmen wanted tougher **Reconstruction** laws. They wanted new Southern leaders. And they wanted equal rights for the **freedmen**.

In 1866, **Congress** voted to keep the Freedmen's Bureau active. And it passed the Civil Rights Bill. This law gave freedmen the same rights as white men, including the right to vote.

Johnson **vetoed** both laws. He felt that they violated states' rights. And he felt that only white men should manage the South.

For the first time in history, Congress voted against presidential vetoes. The Civil Rights Bill and the Freedmen's Bureau Act became law.

Congress also protected the Civil Rights Bill in a new constitutional **amendment**. The Fourteenth Amendment made all African Americans U.S. citizens. It also protected their constitutional rights. Johnson fought the amendment, but lost.

In 1867, Congress passed the first Reconstruction Acts. New Southern state governments had to be elected. All

Southern states had to approve state constitutions that guaranteed voting rights for all men. And they had to approve the Fourteenth **Amendment**.

Congress used the U.S. Army to enforce its new **Reconstruction** laws. **Secretary of War** Edwin Stanton, a **cabinet** member, controlled the army. He made sure it enforced Congress' laws.

Congress feared that President Johnson would interfere with their Reconstruction plans by removing Stanton from office. To protect Stanton, Congress passed the Tenure of Office Bill. This law prevented the president from removing cabinet members without Senate approval.

Edwin Stanton

Johnson **vetoed** this bill. He felt it violated the powers of the president granted by the Constitution. But Congress voted against the veto. The Tenure of Office Bill became law.

The Seven "Hats" of the U.S. President

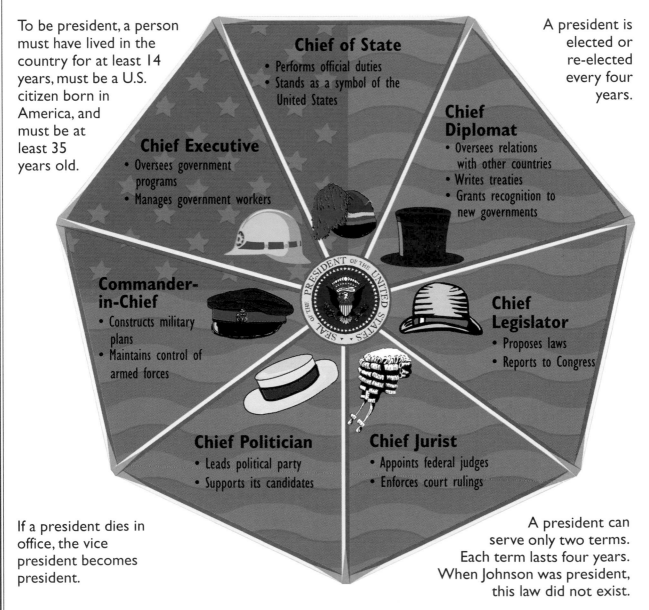

To be president, a person must have lived in the country for at least 14 years, must be a U.S. citizen born in America, and must be at least 35 years old.

A president is elected or re-elected every four years.

Chief of State
- Performs official duties
- Stands as a symbol of the United States

Chief Diplomat
- Oversees relations with other countries
- Writes treaties
- Grants recognition to new governments

Chief Executive
- Oversees government programs
- Manages government workers

Commander-in-Chief
- Constructs military plans
- Maintains control of armed forces

Chief Legislator
- Proposes laws
- Reports to Congress

Chief Politician
- Leads political party
- Supports its candidates

Chief Jurist
- Appoints federal judges
- Enforces court rulings

If a president dies in office, the vice president becomes president.

A president can serve only two terms. Each term lasts four years. When Johnson was president, this law did not exist.

As president, Andrew Johnson had seven jobs.

The Three Branches of the U.S. Government

Congress is in the Capitol Building in Washington, D.C. It can pass laws and stop the president's veto. Congress also can change the Constitution to stop the president's plans or Supreme Court rulings.

The president lives in the White House in Washington, D.C. He or she can stop (veto) laws passed by Congress, and propose new laws. The president also can choose Supreme Court judges.

The Supreme Court is in the Supreme Court Building in Washington, D.C. It can stop laws passed by Congress. It also can change or stop the president's plans.

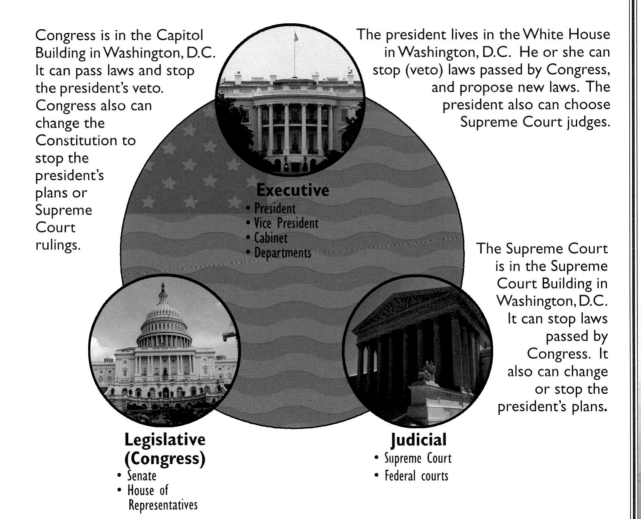

Executive
- President
- Vice President
- Cabinet
- Departments

Legislative (Congress)
- Senate
- House of Representatives

Judicial
- Supreme Court
- Federal courts

The U.S. Constitution formed three government branches. Each branch has power over the others. So, no single group or person can control the country. The Constitution calls this "separation of powers."

Impeachment

*J*ohnson felt a duty to save the South from the hurtful laws of **Congress**. To do this, he needed to take control of the army from Stanton.

Stanton was part of Johnson's **cabinet**. Yet Stanton was not against Congress' **Reconstruction** laws, which Johnson called unconstitutional. Johnson felt Stanton was disloyal. On August 12, 1867, Johnson fired Stanton.

Congress was outraged. They claimed that Johnson violated the Tenure of Office Act. Congress voted to **impeach** President Johnson.

The impeachment trial began in the U.S. Senate on March 30, 1868. Johnson's lawyers claimed that the Tenure of Office Act was unconstitutional. They also claimed that Johnson had the right to "disagree" with Congress.

On May 16, the fifty-four-member Senate voted Johnson's fate. By law, two-thirds (thirty-six) of the senators had to vote guilty to remove Johnson from office. Thirty-five senators voted guilty. Nineteen voted not guilty. President Johnson won by one vote.

After the trial, President Johnson continued to argue with **Congress** over its **Reconstruction** Acts. He also wanted to serve another term. But the **Democratic** party was unwilling to take a chance on him.

The Democrats chose former New York governor Horatio Seymour to run for president. But Ulysses S. Grant, a **Republican**, won the election. Andrew Johnson left the White House on March 3, 1869.

Andrew Johnson's impeachment by the U.S. Congress

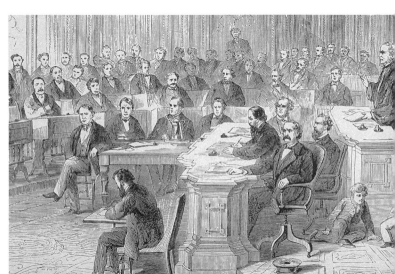

After the White House

*J*ohnson and his family returned home to Greeneville, Tennessee. They worked to rebuild their house. Like many homes in the South, the Johnson house was badly damaged from the battles fought during the **Civil War**.

Johnson stayed interested in politics. In 1872, he ran for the Tennessee senate, but lost. He was elected to the U.S. Senate in 1875. He is the only former president to become a senator.

A few months later, Johnson became very sick. On July 31, 1875, he died. Andrew Johnson was buried with a copy of the U.S. Constitution as his pillow.

A presidential portrait of Andrew Johnson

28

Fun Facts

- In March 1867, Secretary of State William Seward arranged the purchase of Russian America in a treaty with the Russians. The new territory was called Alaska. **Congress** approved the treaty. But newspapers criticized the purchase. They called it "Seward's Folly." They also called it "Johnson's polar bear garden" because the land was cold and wild.

- The first time Eliza McCardle saw Andrew Johnson, she told a friend he was her "beau," or boyfriend, even though she had not met him yet. Soon after, they fell in love and were married.

- When Johnson returned to the U.S. Senate after his presidency, he was welcomed with a bouquet of flowers on his desk.

Glossary

acquit - to declare not guilty.

amendment - a change to the Constitution of the United States.

apprentice - a person who learns a trade or craft from a skilled worker.

avenge - to get even with someone.

cabinet - a group of advisers chosen by the president.

Civil War - The war between the Union and Confederate States of America from 1861 to 1865.

Confederacy - the eleven states that left the U.S. during the Civil War.

Congress - the lawmaking body of the U.S. It is made up of the Senate and the House of Representatives.

debate - to discuss a question or topic.

Democrat - one of the political parties of the U.S. During the Civil War, Democrats were conservative and supported farming.

federal - the national government of the U.S.

freedmen - freed African American slaves.

House of Representatives - a group of people elected by citizens to represent them. They meet in Washington, D.C., to make laws for the nation. Most states also have a House of Representatives to make state laws.

impeach - to have a trial to decide if the president should be removed from office.

Reconstruction - the period of time after the Civil War when laws were passed to help the Southern states rebuild, and return to the Union.

repeal - to remove a law or decision.

Republican - one of the political parties of the U.S. During the Civil War, Republicans were liberal and against slavery.

secede - to break away from a group.

Secretary of War - an adviser to the president who handles the nation's defense.

tailor - a person who makes clothes.

Union - the states that remained in the U.S. during the Civil War. Also, the United States of America.

veto - to keep a law or vote from passing. Veto is a special power held by the president. Congress can overrule a veto with a two-thirds majority vote.

Internet Sites

The Presidents of the United States of America
http://www.whitehouse.gov/WH/glimpse/presidents/html/presidents.html
This site is from the White House. With an introduction from President Bill Clinton and biographies that include each president's inaugural address, this site is excellent. Get information on White House history, art in the White House, first ladies, first families, and much more.

POTUS—Presidents of the United States
http://www.ipl.org/ref/POTUS/
In this resource you will find background information, election results, cabinet members, presidency highlights, and some odd facts on each of the presidents. Links to biographies, historical documents, audio and video files, and other presidential sites are also included to enrich this site.

These sites are subject to change. Go to your favorite search engine and type in United States presidents for more sites.

Pass It On

History enthusiasts: educate readers around the country by passing on information you've learned about presidents or other important people who've changed history. Share your little-known facts and interesting stories. We want to hear from you!

To get posted on the ABDO Publishing Company Web site, email us at:
history@abdopub.com
Visit the ABDO Publishing Company Web site at www.abdopub.com

Index

DISCARD

		DATE	